Getting to Know God

Sandra Williamson
The Spirit Realm Series

Getting to Know God
Print Book ISBN - 978-1-947426-98-6
Ebook ISBN - 978-1-947426-97-9

Copyright © 2019 by Sandra Willamson

Published by Winters Publishing Group

Book development and editing services by Winters Publishing Group

Dedication

This book is dedicated to all God's children who want to know Him in a personal, even tangible way. God is just waiting for you to come close!

Did you ever wonder what God is like? God wants you to get to know Him! He wants you to know how He thinks, acts, and feels. God is your friend!

God is actually three persons, the Father God, the Son Jesus, and the Holy Spirit. They all think exactly the same – they just have different jobs.

God is the one that made everything that you see – the world, the plants and trees, the animals – and even you.

God already knows all about You. Did you know that? He loves everything about you, because He is the one that made you before you were born! You were made to be a part of God's family.

He made you as a spirit (that is the part of you that lives forever just like God), then He put you in a body, and He gave you a soul. Your soul is the part of you that thinks, and feels, and likes to play!

You can get to know God and all about how He made you by reading His story book. It is called *The Bible*. You will find all kinds of stories in the Bible about how people got to know God and how they became His friend.

Jesus loves to tell His story to you! He will speak right to your heart while you are reading! It is like a whisper in your ear, but it is not out loud. You may barely hear His voice, but deep inside you will know that you heard Him!

You can also get to know Him by talking right to Him! Most of the time this is called "prayer." Prayer is just talking to God and listening to what He is saying back to you!

Do you know that you can see God while you pray?

God is a Spirit, that is why we don't see Him as easily as we see other things. To see Him, we have to decide to think the way God thinks and see things the way God sees them. We do that with the Spirit part of who we are.

When you are praying and talking to Father God, the best thing to do is to imagine His face and see Him smiling at you! Start by using your imagination to make a picture in your mind, then Father God will show you how to see Him.

Do you see Father God? Father God's home is in Heaven and He sits on a big throne. Can you see Him in your mind? He wants you to come close to Him and talk to Him. Close your eyes, it will help.

Father God doesn't want you to be far away from Him, He wants you to come close, very, very close!

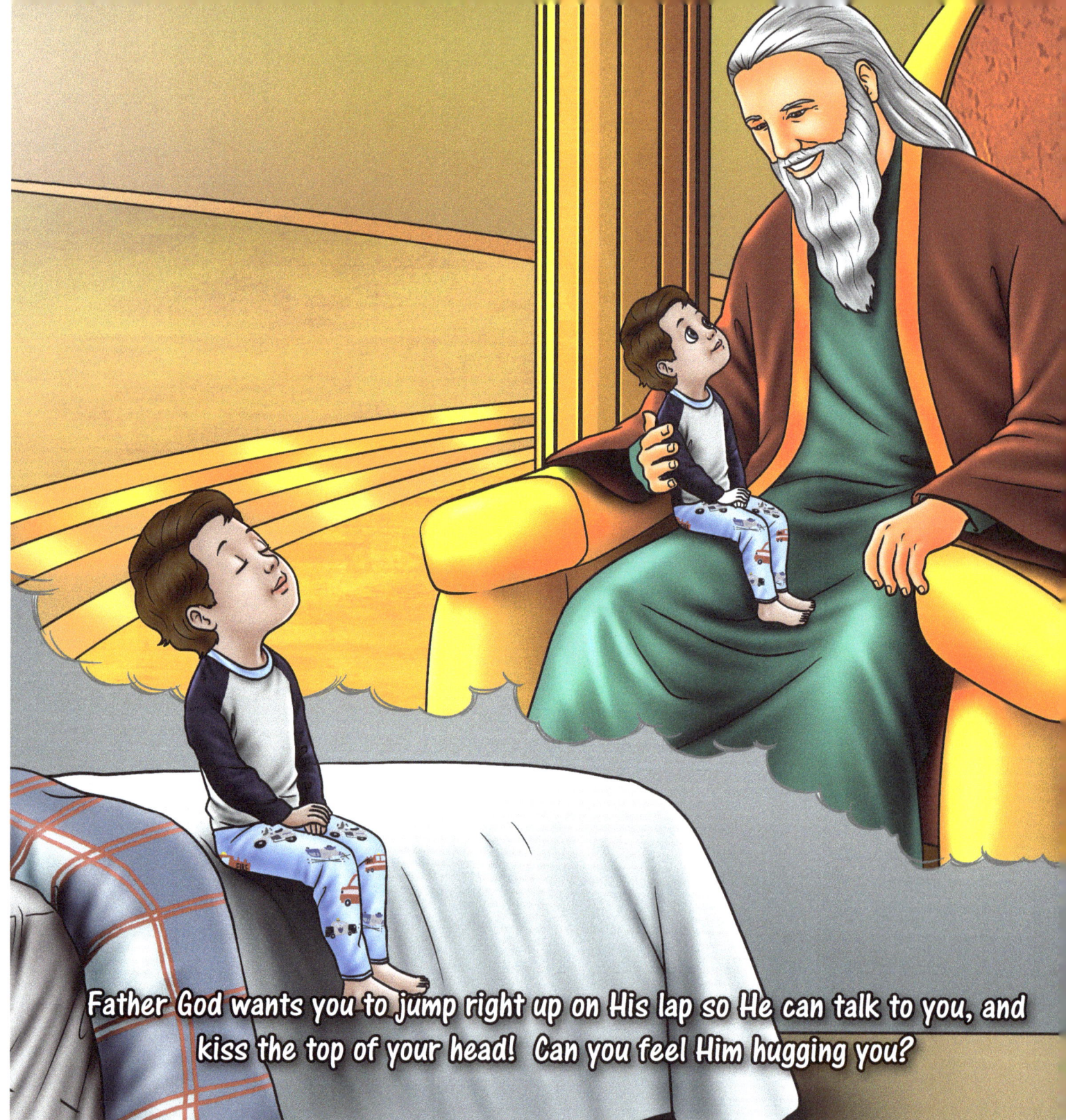

Father God wants you to jump right up on His lap so He can talk to you, and kiss the top of your head! Can you feel Him hugging you?

Like a loving Daddy here on Earth, Father God wants you to come to Him all the time to talk to Him and to let Him show you His love. He misses you if you do not come to talk to Him! Go to Father God every day and talk to Him often!

Now let's pray again and see Jesus. Jesus, the Son of God, has promised He will always be with you. That means right now, wherever you are!

In His story book, the Bible, it tells us that He is "closer than a brother." That means He is always right there, right where you are, probably with His arm around your shoulders! Now close your eyes and see where Jesus is, right next to you!

Jesus wants you to talk to Him about all your thoughts, all your decisions, and even all your troubles. He wants to help you make good decisions and help you to always be joyful and happy!

Close your eyes and see if you can see where Jesus is – is He behind you?
Is He next to you with His arm around you? Or is He right in front of you
smiling as He looks into your eyes?

Isn't it fun to see Jesus and to talk to Him? He is the best friend ever!

The Holy Spirit wants you to know Him too! He wants you to know He is like a warm, fuzzy blanket that covers you and protects you. His job is to teach you God's ways. The Holy Spirit spends time with you any time you ask Him to come.

When you talk to the Holy Spirit, ask Him to come and let you feel His presence, His goodness, and His care for you. He is like your parents when they make sure you are cozy in your bed at night, that you eat good food, and that you go to school to learn. The Holy Spirit wants to teach you all about the good things of God!

Close your eyes and ask the Holy Spirit to bring you His Peace and Comfort and to show you some wonderful things about God and what God has planned for your life!

His presence is so comforting and loving! Thank you, Holy Spirit, for coming and teaching me!

The best part of learning to see Father God, Jesus, and the Holy Spirit is that you can see them and talk to them any time you want. They are always right there listening and waiting for you.

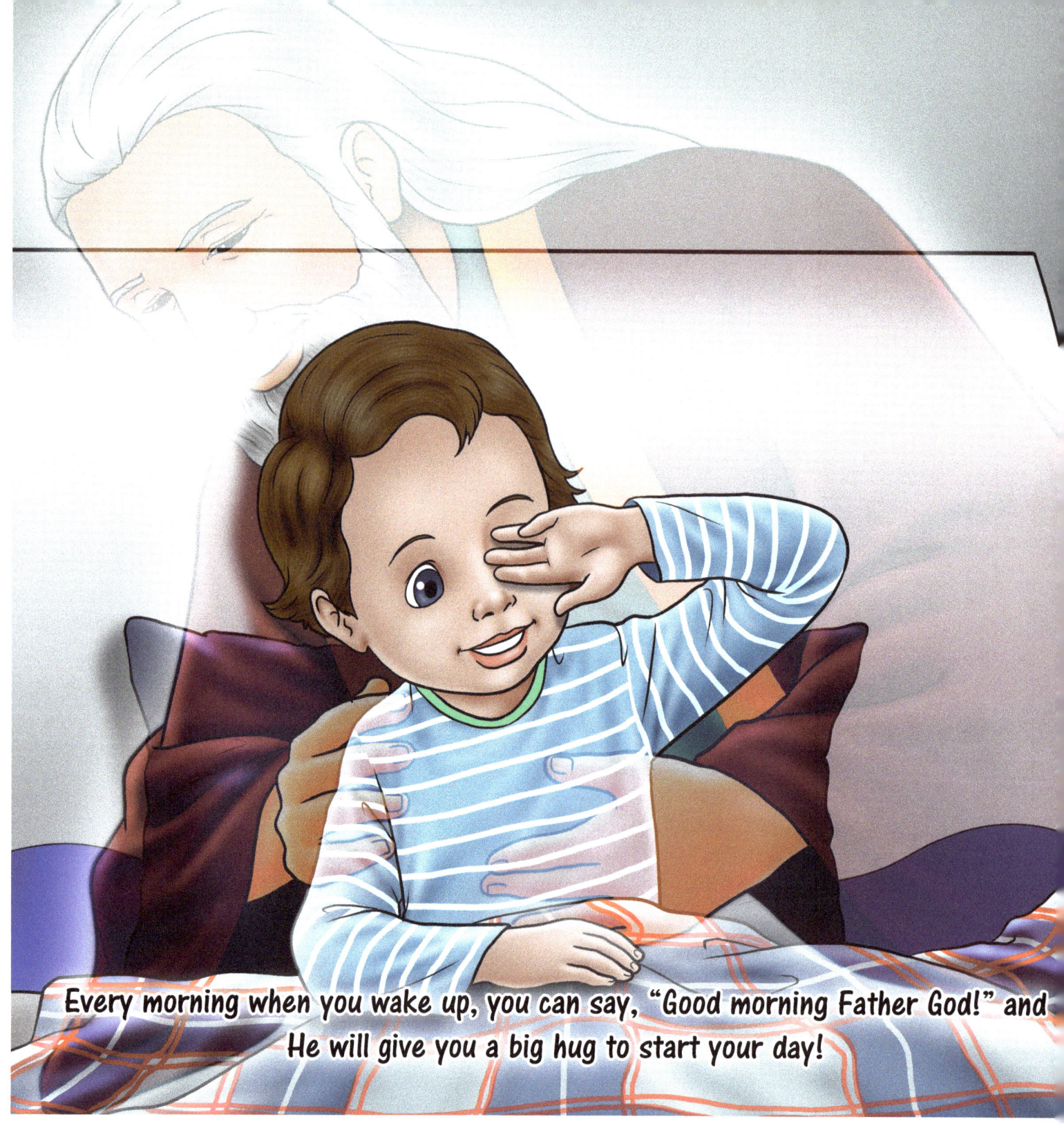

Every morning when you wake up, you can say, "Good morning Father God!" and He will give you a big hug to start your day!

When you get ready to go out to play or to school, ask Jesus to go have fun with you. He will always be there, and you can talk to Him as you go!

And when you need help, when you can't find your favorite toy, or you need to remember where you put your shoes, guess who will help you if you ask Him? That's right! The Holy Spirit is always ready to give you guidance in everything you do!

God is so wonderful, and He wants you to be part of His family, forever!
Just ask Him!

How to become part of God's Family Forever

Say this prayer with all your heart:

"Dear Father God, Jesus, and Holy Spirit, I want to be a part of your family. You said in the Bible that if I believe in You with my whole heart and believe that everything You did for me was to give me eternal life, and that if I accept You, Jesus, as Lord of my life, I would be Your child forever.

So, Father God, I now say that I believe in You, I believe in Jesus Christ who is my best friend, and I believe in the Holy Spirit who is always here to help me. Please forgive me for all the bad things (called sin) that I have done. I accept Jesus now as my Lord and Savior, which means He has saved me from evil and sin. I accept my salvation right now!

Thank You, Father God, for forgiving me, saving me, and giving me eternal life with You. Amen!"

Other books from the Author

The "Do You See Them?" series:

Book #1 "Do You See Them?"
In the Garden

It all began in the Garden, where God made a special place to walk and talk with His most precious creation, mandkind. Everything was beautiful and God and His people loved living together in God's beautiful creation. But an evil enemy had plans to ruin the family of God before it had barely begun!
Look and see as God's plan is revealed!

Book #2 "Do You See Them?"
Learning God's Ways

The classic stories tell of all manner of miracles. What if you could see behind the scenes the roles the angels played? Daniel surely wasn't alone in the lion's den; Shadrach, Mesheck and Abendigo absolutely had unseen help in the fiery furnace?; and Jonah in the whale was clearly preserved at the Lord's instruction. Read and discover!

Book #3 "Do You See Them?"
I See Jesus!

This book reveals Jesus and His amazing miracles, the people that He touched, and how Satan tried to stop Him. Father God sent His Son to demonstrate Heaven coming to earth. A spiritual upheaval takes place as the world submits to the Lord's commands! look and see!

Book#4- "Do You See Them?"
God Wants to Use Me!

The fourth book in this series shows how God used ordinary people to do extraordinary things! Follow Peter and Paul as they speak healing to the lame man, preach the Good News, and teach the new church how to follow Jesus! Courage and strength in the Lord are learned in these New Testament stories that reveal just how many of God's helpers are surrounding us all the time. Say "Yes" and go!

Book#5- "Do You See Them?"
The King's Return

One day soon, Jesus will return to the earth. He is coming for His people, and He is zealous to bring His people, His Bride, to His Kingdom! Jesus comes to rescue His people from the hands of the enemy, once and for all! A whirlwind of the power and might of God are seen as the last attempts of the enemy to stop God's people from following Him are finally thwarted! Look up!

We hope you enjoyed the first book in the "Do You See Them?" series. Yet it doesn't end here. As Adam and Eve leave the special Garden, God already had a rescue plan in place. His goodness and kindness is all around them as He begins to teach mankind His ways. The "Do You See Them?" series is a peek into what is already happening all around us, everyday, unseen.

Watch for the next books in the "Do You See Them" series coming soon!

To order copies of the "Do You See Them?" book series, go to:
www.DoYouSeeThem.com or www.SpiritRealmSeries.com

About the Author

Sandra Williamson has a heart for children and delights in teaching them natural and spiritual realities. One of Sandra's greatest joys is to teach children the reality of the Word of God in pictures and stories.

Sandra grew up struggling with issues that could now be attributed to Autism Spectrum Disorders. She was diagnosed with 'brain astigmatism' as an adolescent and was not able to even accomplish high school. While raising her children, Sandra became desperate to find a way to extricate herself from the grasp of the disorder. Through continual prayer and rigorous study, Sandra was able to finish high school at age 28 and went on to pursue higher education. Sandra now holds a bachelor's certification in paralegal studies from California State University, a bachelor's degree in psychology from Oklahoma State University, and master's degree in human relations from the University of Oklahoma.

Sandra is the Founder and Executive Director of an international spiritual freedom and emotional healing ministry, "God's E.R." (*Emergency Restoration*), helping hundreds of individuals each year find the Truth of the Word of God to become healed in the whole person. Sandra's career has been an ongoing combination of ministry and natural support, always with the goal of helping others at the heart of her efforts.

Sandra Williamson is an ordained minister who lives in Tulsa, Oklahoma with her husband, James Williamson. The Williamson's are blessed to have four adult children and five grandchildren. Sandra is the author of the *Do Your See Them?* children series, and *Say, 'Yes!'* (2014), a vision of the Bride of Christ.

www.ingramcontent.com/pod-product-compliance
Lightning Source LLC
LaVergne TN
LVHW070841080426
835513LV00024B/2430